D1293983

# SLAP SHOT

## SYNONYMS AND ANTONYMS

By Anna Prokos
Cover illustrated by Scott Angle
Interior illustrated by Robert Roper
Language arts curriculum consultant: Debra Voege, M.A.

**Gareth Stevens**
Publishing

Please visit our web site at **www.garethstevens.com**.
For a free color catalog describing Gareth Stevens Publishing's list of
high-quality books, call 1-800-542-2595 (USA) or 1-800-387-3178 (Canada).
Gareth Stevens Publishing's fax: 1-877-542-2596

Library of Congress Cataloging-in-Publication Data

Prokos, Anna.
   Slap shot synonyms and antonyms / by Anna Prokos ; illustrated by Robert Roper ;
 language arts curriculum consultant: Debra Voege, M.A.
     p. cm. — (Grammar all-stars: kinds of words)
    At head of title : Grammar all-stars : kinds of words
    Includes bibliographical references and index.
    ISBN-10: 1-4339-0013-0  ISBN-13: 978-1-4339-0013-6 (lib. bdg.)
    ISBN-10: 1-4339-0153-6  ISBN-13: 978-1-4339-0153-9 (pbk.)
    1. English language—Synonyms and antonyms—Juvenile literature.
  2. English language—Grammar—Juvenile literature. I. Voege, Debra.
 II. Title. III. Title: Grammar all-stars : kinds of words.
 PE1591.P76  2008
 428.1—dc22               2008031359

This edition first published in 2009 by
**Gareth Stevens Publishing**
A Weekly Reader® Company
1 Reader's Digest Road
Pleasantville, NY 10570-7000  USA

Copyright © 2009 by Gareth Stevens, Inc.

Executive Managing Editor: Lisa M. Herrington
Senior Editor: Barbara Bakowski
Creative Director: Lisa Donovan
Art Director: Ken Crossland
Publisher: Keith Garton

Printed in the United States of America

1 2 3 4 5 6 7 8 9 10 09 08

# CONTENTS

Look for the **boldface** words on each page.
Then read the **HOCKEY HINT** that follows.

# CHAPTER 1

## FACE-OFF CHALLENGE

### *What Are Synonyms?*

"Welcome, hockey fans! This is Buzz Star, reporting live on P-L-A-Y TV. I'm at Slap Shot Stadium for the **last** game of the playoffs. In this **final** match, the Midville Mighty Pucks are facing off against the Baytown Blades."

A boy joins Buzz in the broadcast booth. "Kid reporter Harold Hattrick will help me with the play-by-play," Buzz says. "Harold won a hockey shoot-out for kids. He was the **top** scorer on the junior league's **best** team."

"I blasted my winning shot **under** the goalie's pads," Harold recalls. "He didn't see the puck **beneath** him in the net."

"Harold, who is your favorite player?" Buzz asks.

"My hero is the Mighty Pucks captain, Dwayne Greatzky," Harold replies. "But I don't see him on the ice yet."

"The game is about to **begin**. It looks as if the Mighty Pucks will have to **start** without their captain," Buzz says. "Greatzky took a hard check in last night's game. He might stay on the bench tonight."

"The Mighty Pucks may need his help to win the game. The **Chilly** Cup is one **cool** trophy!" Harold exclaims.

"Harold, you just used a pair of synonyms!" says Buzz.

"Oh, sorry," Harold says. "I didn't mean to. I don't even know what a cinnamon— I mean, *synonym*—is."

"No need to be sorry," Buzz replies. "Synonyms are words that have the same meaning, like **start** and **begin** or **chilly** and **cool**."

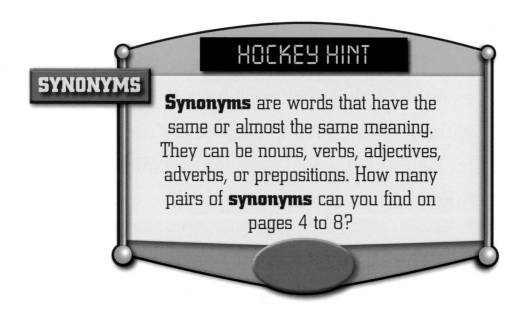

**SYNONYMS**

**HOCKEY HINT**

**Synonyms** are words that have the same or almost the same meaning. They can be nouns, verbs, adjectives, adverbs, or prepositions. How many pairs of **synonyms** can you find on pages 4 to 8?

Buzz starts the play-by-play. "The Blades win the face-off. Left wing Flash Wiggins has the puck."

Harold takes over. "Wiggins skates **quickly** down the ice. He sees that Blades center Skid Crossley is wide open. Wiggins **rapidly** passes him the puck. Crossley skates **speedily** toward the goal."

"Mighty Pucks defender Redd Lyne **shadows** Crossley," adds Buzz. "Lyne **trails** closely to keep up with his opponent. Wiggins **follows** Crossley, too. Crossley makes a drop pass."

"The Mighty Pucks defenders close in on Wiggins at the blue line," Harold says. "Somehow he squeezes between them."

"That's a **hard** move!" Buzz exclaims.
"Splitting the defense is **tough**. Now
Wiggins is on a fast break. He raises his
stick for a **tricky** slap shot."

"He scores!" Harold shouts.

"The Baytown Blades strike first with a **big** goal. Will they take a **large** lead?" Buzz asks. "Or will the Midville Mighty Pucks make a **huge** comeback in the second period?"

"And will Dwayne Greatzky take the ice to help his team?" Harold wonders.

"That's the end of the first period," Buzz says. "After the break, we'll return to the Chilly Cup finals. Stay tuned, folks!"

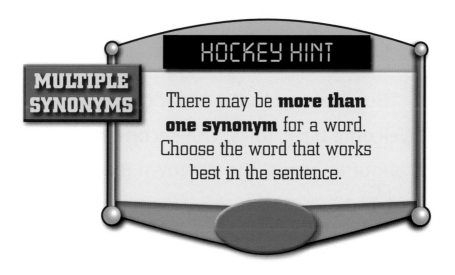

HOCKEY HINT

MULTIPLE SYNONYMS

There may be **more than one synonym** for a word. Choose the word that works best in the sentence.

# UP AND DOWN THE ICE

## *What Are Antonyms?*

"Flash Wiggins makes scoring look **easy**," Harold tells Buzz. "But beating the goalie is **difficult**. Wiggins has a **strong** slap shot. He wouldn't score many goals if his shot were **weak**."

Buzz returns to the broadcast. "Welcome back, folks. The second period is about to begin. The Baytown Blades lead 1–0."

"The Mighty Pucks may be at a **loss** without Dwayne Greatzky," Harold adds. "To get a **win**, they'll need their star player."

"There's no sign of Greatzky," says Buzz. "But the Mighty Pucks coach is making some changes to the first line. Connie Smythe will play **right** wing. Stanley Krupp takes over at **left** wing."

"Smythe **always** plays a clean game," Harold says. "Krupp **never** loses control of the puck. They could keep the Blades from scoring again."

"Krupp is ready for the face-off," Buzz says. "He lines up opposite Deke Decker."

"The referee drops the puck. Decker wins the face-off," Harold reports. "He skates along the boards. Decker tries a wraparound **behind** the goal post. But Mighty Pucks defender Sal Sniper gets the puck. He flicks it **ahead** to center ice."

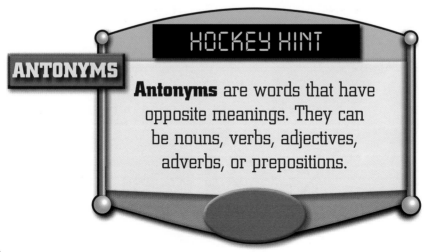

HOCKEY HINT

ANTONYMS

**Antonyms** are words that have opposite meanings. They can be nouns, verbs, adjectives, adverbs, or prepositions.

"Now Krupp takes control of the puck and feeds it to Smythe," Buzz says. "The two players pass **back** and **forth**."

"Krupp flips a wrist shot toward the net!" Harold exclaims.

"The Blades goalie stops the puck just **outside** the crease," Buzz says. "But Smythe is there for the rebound. He taps it **inside** the net! It's a goal!"

"Krupp and Smythe worked **together** to even the score," Harold adds. "Nothing can tear them **apart**!"

The period goes on with fast breaks, line changes, and power plays—but no goals. When the buzzer sounds, the score remains tied.

"Let's go to a commercial as the Zamboni clears the ice," Buzz says. "We'll be back after this message."

Harold heads **down** to the ice. "Can I catch a ride on the Zamboni?" he asks. The driver nods. Harold climbs **up** to sit beside him.

"You can help me make this **rough** ice **smooth** again!" says the driver.

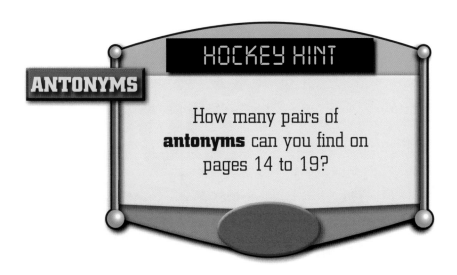

**HOCKEY HINT**

**ANTONYMS**

How many pairs of **antonyms** can you find on pages 14 to 19?

As Harold winds his way around the rink, Buzz talks to a few fans in the stands.

"Which team will **win**?" he asks.

"The Mighty Pucks can't **lose**!" one girl says. "They won't be **defeated**!"

"What do you think of the game so far?" Buzz asks a man in a Blades jersey.

"This is the **best** hockey I've ever seen!" the fan replies. "Last season, the Blades had the **worst** record. This year, they have the **finest** team in the league."

"The third period will be a nail-biter," Buzz predicts. "The Chilly Cup is at stake!"

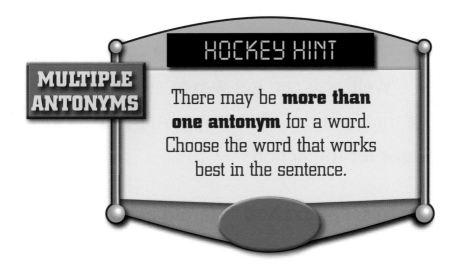

**MULTIPLE ANTONYMS**

**HOCKEY HINT**

There may be **more than one antonym** for a word. Choose the word that works best in the sentence.

# CHAPTER 3

## LAST SHOT FOR FIRST PLACE

### *Using Synonyms and Antonyms*

"How was your Zamboni ride?" Buzz asks his kid reporter when they return to the press box.

"It was like riding a big lawn mower," Harold replies excitedly. "Except it was really **cold**!"

"Well, you can get **warm** as we cover the third period," Buzz says. "Are you **eager** for the action?"

"Yes, I'm **excited**," Harold answers.

Suddenly, the crowd gives a loud cheer. "I think the Mighty Pucks fans are thrilled, too. They just spotted Dwayne Greatzky skating onto the ice!" Harold adds.

"Let's update any viewers who just tuned in," Buzz says. "It is the **last** period of the **final** playoff game. Mighty Pucks star Dwayne Greatzky has come off the bench."

"Greatzky was **hurt** in Game 6," Harold explains. "Even though he is **injured**, he'll try to help his team snap a 1–1 tie."

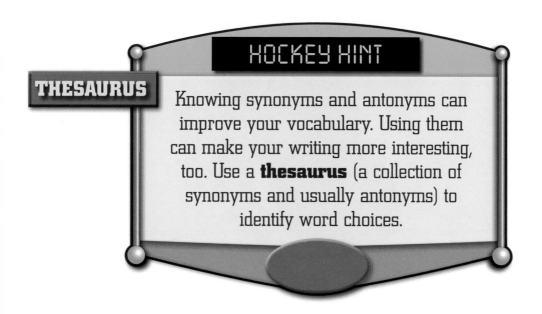

**THESAURUS**

HOCKEY HINT

Knowing synonyms and antonyms can improve your vocabulary. Using them can make your writing more interesting, too. Use a **thesaurus** (a collection of synonyms and usually antonyms) to identify word choices.

"And Greatzky **wins** the face-off," Buzz reports. "He makes an **excellent** pass to Sal Sniper. Oh, Sniper **loses** control of the puck! That's a **bad** turnover for the Mighty Pucks."

"The Blades are playing **good** defense," Harold notes. "The Mighty Pucks won't score unless they make some **great** shots."

After almost a full period of play, the score remains tied. "Time is running out, folks," Buzz says. "**Both** teams are hoping for a goal before the buzzer. **Neither** coach wants to go to overtime."

"Several players are scrambling for the puck," says Harold. "Flash Wiggins **takes** control. He winds up for a slap shot. Wiggins **gives** it his all, but the shot rings off the post."

"Stanley Krupp clears the puck," Buzz continues. "He spots Greatzky and sends him a **quick** pass. With just five seconds left, Greatzky fires a **swift** wrist shot."

"The puck sails **above** the goalie's shoulder and just **below** the crossbar. Score!" Harold shouts. "The Midville Mighty Pucks have won the game!"

The **winners** crowd around Dwayne Greatzky. "We wouldn't be **champions** without you, Dwayne!" Krupp says.

Greatzky accepts the **prize** for his team. He raises the **trophy** above his head. Then he **calmly** skates in a circle around the ice. The fans cheer **wildly**.

Buzz and Harold head down to center ice. "How does it feel to be the **Chilly** Cup champs?" Buzz asks Greatzky.

"Very **cool**!" he replies.

"But the Mighty Pucks and the Blades should share this trophy," Greatzky adds. He asks the Baytown Blades to join him on the ice. "Your team is a lot like ours. Let's make one new team out of our two teams."

Skid Crossley smiles. "If you can't beat 'em, join 'em," he replies. "What would we call our new team?"

Harold chimes in. "How about the Same Differences?"

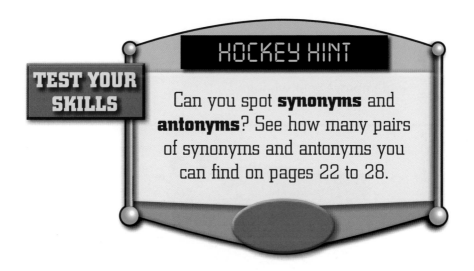

**TEST YOUR SKILLS**

**HOCKEY HINT**

Can you spot **synonyms** and **antonyms**? See how many pairs of synonyms and antonyms you can find on pages 22 to 28.

# BUZZ STAR PLAYS BY THE RULES!

 **Synonyms** are words that have the same or almost the same meanings. Synonyms can be nouns, verbs, adjectives, adverbs, or prepositions.

**Examples:**   winner, champion    start, begin        big, large
                 quickly, rapidly    beneath, below

 A word can have more than one **synonym**.
**Examples:** difficult, hard, tough, tricky

 **Antonyms** are words that have opposite meanings. Antonyms can be nouns, verbs, adjectives, adverbs, or prepositions.

**Examples:**   winner, loser       come, go           weak, strong
                 always, never       over, under

 A word can have more than one **antonym**.
**Examples:** begin: end, finish, complete, conclude

 Look in a **thesaurus** (a collection of synonyms and usually antonyms) to identify word choices. You can build your vocabulary and improve your writing.

# ALL-STAR ACTIVITY

Harold wrote an article for his youth team's web site.
On a piece of paper, **write the best synonym** for each underlined word.

SEARCH SITE | ◀FLAG SITE

## MIGHTY PUCKS

I was at Game 7 of the <u>final</u> (last, middle) round in the Chilly Cup championship. The fans cheered <u>loudly</u> (happily, noisily) as the teams took the ice. It was a <u>thrilling</u> (exciting, solid) game!

The Baytown Blades <u>quickly</u> (rapidly, easily) scored the <u>first</u> (trickiest, earliest) goal. The Midville Mighty Pucks were playing without the <u>injured</u> (famous, hurt) Dwayne Greatzky.

After two periods, the score was <u>tied</u> (equal, huge). <u>Finally</u> (at last, oddly), Greatzky came off the bench. His last-minute goal <u>gave</u> (surprised, provided) the Mighty Pucks a big <u>win</u> (victory, failure)!

Skid Crossley said it was the <u>toughest</u> (most difficult, longest) game he has ever played. He was <u>disappointed</u> (saddened, eager) that his team lost.

Greatzky asked the Blades to <u>join</u> (celebrate, unite) the <u>winners</u> (champions, fans). The players are going to <u>create</u> (form, quit) a <u>new</u> (former, fresh) team.

### All-Star Challenge

Write an **antonym** for each underlined word in the article.

Turn the page to check your answers and to see how many points you scored!

# ANSWER KEY

## Did you find enough synonyms to win the Chilly Cup?

**0–4** synonyms: Offsides

**5–8** synonyms: Penalty

**9–12** synonyms: Assist

**13–16** synonyms: GOAL!

### SYNONYMS

1. last
2. noisily
3. exciting
4. rapidly
5. earliest
6. hurt
7. equal
8. at last
9. provided
10. victory
11. most difficult
12. saddened
13. unite
14. champions
15. form
16. fresh

### All-Star Challenge

Note: These are possible answers. There may be more than one correct antonym.

1. first
2. quietly
3. boring
4. slowly
5. last
6. unharmed
7. uneven
8. initially
9. took away
10. defeat
11. easiest
12. satisfied
13. separate
14. losers
15. destroy
16. old